P9-BJC-215

Mark J. Asher

BARK &
RIDE

a tail-wagging adventure

Andrews McMeel
Publishing

Kansas City

06 07 08 09 10 SDB 10 9 8 7 6 5 4 3 2 1

ISBN-13: 978-0-7407-5703-7
ISBN-10: 0-7407-5703-2
Library of Congress Control Number: 2005931542

www.andrewsmcmeel.com

Designed by Gayle Chin

Attention: Schools and Businesses
Andrews McMeel books are available at quantity discounts with bulk
purchase for educational, business, or sales promotional use. For
information, please write to: Special Sales Department, Andrews
McMeel Publishing, 4520 Main Street, Kansas City, Missouri 64111.

Thank You

Zan Nix, Rock-N-Rolla's Café in Ashland, Rogue Valley Transportation District, Terry Lomis, A Taste of Honey Limousine Service, Cycle Optics, Westlake Village Golf Course, Jesse Hanwit, Gayle Chin, Speedway Granny, Ashland Police Department, 4 Paws on 5th Ave.

Imagine if dogs could drive.

We'd cruise to the beach . . .

and smell the sweet salt air.

We'd catch a canine cab to the dog park.

We'd drive real slow to check out cute dogs.

We'd ride without constraints.

SLOWER
DOGS
KEEP
RIGHT

We'd pull over to watch beautiful sunsets.

We'd go to golf courses that allow paws on the green.

We'd ride in fire-engine red classic cars.

We'd plow the fields looking for buried treasures.

We'd get behind the wheel at six months old.

We'd pull over and chow down at our favorite burger joint.

We'd stop to fix any trouble under the hood.

We'd pick up our friends and head to agility training.

We'd be out hitching a ride.

We'd read the morning paper and enjoy a cup of joe.

We'd hit the slopes.

We'd drive the trolley car into town . . .

and take our friends shopping for bones and chew toys.

We'd use the glove box as a fold-out bed.

We'd meditate deeply in the backseat.

We'd ride three-wheelers through the forest.

We'd sell ice cream during the dog days of summer.

We'd take our owners out for a ride.

We'd ride the wind by day . . .

and by night.

We'd cruise out to the lake and see if the fish were biting.

IF YOU CAN READ THIS
TURN ME OVER

7

7

BLACKWELL AUTO

We'd race cars built just for us.

We'd scan the landscape for stray cats.

We'd watch the world go by.

We'd patrol the streets for deadbeat dog owners.

Then we'd fall asleep on the job.

We'd take our mate on a date.

We'd drive our pampered friends around in style.

PARKING
FOR
LIMOS
ONLY

Occasionally, we'd reluctantly clean up the dog hair.

We'd face dreary days in stylish rain gear.

We'd hit the open road.